Birds

By Sally Cowan

T0360150

There are many sorts
of birds.

Most birds can fly and glide.

They can chirp and sing
and quack, too!

Birds fly with their wings.

First, a bird jumps up
to take off.

Then it flaps its wings.

But emus are birds that can not fly.

Their home is on the red dirt.

Birds fly high to look
for things to eat.

Some birds sip from plants.

Their long beaks can reach
inside buds.

Birds stir up dirt to find things to eat, too.

Birds can eat bugs, moths and ants.

Some big birds hunt fish.

They can grab the fish
with their feet.

This bird sits in a fir tree
and looks for things to eat.

It will fly and whirl to grab
a snack!

Birds can make nests in trees.

First, they pick up twigs
and sticks.

Then they twirl in feathers and fluffy things to make the nest.

They lay eggs in the nest.

Birds' eggs crack in spring.

The hungry chicks peek out.

They cheep and chirp!

Big birds feed the chicks
with their beaks.

If we put a dish in the garden,
a bird might come for a drink!

It can have a splash!

CHECKING FOR MEANING

1. What sort of bird lives in the red dirt? *(Literal)*

2. At what time of the year do birds' eggs hatch? *(Literal)*

3. Why do you think birds fly high to look for things to eat? *(Inferential)*

EXTENDING VOCABULARY

chirp	What other words have a similar meaning to *chirp*? Can you think of any other animals that chirp? E.g. crickets.
whirl	What does it mean if a bird *whirls* to grab a snack? Why do you think the author chose to use this word?
twigs	How are *twigs* different from *sticks*? How is it similar? Where might you find twigs?

MOVING BEYOND THE TEXT

1. What other animals live in trees?

2. What do you think is important for a bird to do when making a nest?

3. Why might people choose to keep a bird as a pet?

4. What sorts of birds can be found where you live?

SPEED SOUNDS

ar	er	ir	ur	or

PRACTICE WORDS

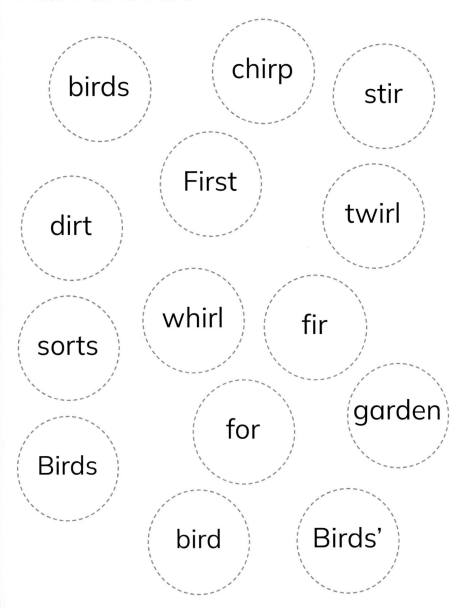

birds

chirp

stir

First

dirt

twirl

whirl

fir

sorts

garden

Birds

for

bird

Birds'